India Before Buddha And The Faith And Philosophy Of His Time

Sir Hari Singh Gour

Kessinger Publishing's Rare Reprints

Thousands of Scarce and Hard-to-Find Books on These and other Subjects!

- Americana
- Ancient Mysteries
- Animals
- Anthropology
- Architecture
- Arts
- Astrology
- Bibliographies
- Biographies & Memoirs
- Body, Mind & Spirit
- Business & Investing
- Children & Young Adult
- Collectibles
- Comparative Religions
- Crafts & Hobbies
- Earth Sciences
- Education
- Ephemera
- Fiction
- Folklore
- Geography
- Health & Diet
- History
- Hobbies & Leisure
- Humor
- Illustrated Books
- Language & Culture
- Law
- Life Sciences

- Literature
- Medicine & Pharmacy
- Metaphysical
- Music
- Mystery & Crime
- Mythology
- Natural History
- Outdoor & Nature
- Philosophy
- Poetry
- Political Science
- Science
- Psychiatry & Psychology
- Reference
- Religion & Spiritualism
- Rhetoric
- Sacred Books
- Science Fiction
- Science & Technology
- Self-Help
- Social Sciences
- Symbolism
- Theatre & Drama
- Theology
- Travel & Explorations
- War & Military
- Women
- Yoga
- *Plus Much More!*

**We kindly invite you to view our catalog list at:
http://www.kessinger.net**

Because this article has been extracted from a parent book, it may have non-pertinent text at the beginning or end of it.

Any blank pages following the article are necessary for our book production requirements. The article herein is complete.

CHAPTER II.

India, north of the Ganges, is an extensive plain. In fact, if one travels from Lahore to Calcutta, one seldom sees a hill. It is in this fertile plain, watered by the Indus and the other rivers in the Punjab, the Ganges and the Jamna and their numerous tributaries in the area now known as the United Provinces of Agra and Oudh, and in the Province of Bihar that the first hordes of the Aryan immigrants from the passes on the north and the north-west settled down. And it is here that the scene of early Buddhism was enacted. This vast plain, in Buddhist times, was sparsely populated : its population all told could not have exceeded twenty millions. There were only a dozen towns of any importance—the rest of the country was dotted with villages, in which the inhabitants followed their rustic occupation of farming and husbandry. The staple crops grown by them were wheat and rice, the latter in watery areas such as the Terai of the Himalyas where the annual rainfall is collected by these mighty barriers on the north and poured down into the plain below, inundating the fields and manuring them with their periodical wash-aways. The northern tracts of the United Provinces and Bihar are thus fertile valleys for the growth of rice, and Buddh's father and family were engaged in the raising of the crop. This part of the country was then covered with forest ; only cultivation clearances had been made, and the villages and the fields were surrounded by the forests of primeval growth, which disappeared with the increasing pressure of population.

When Buddhism arose. there was no paramount sovereign in India([1]). It was ruled by republics and monarchies of which four were of considerable size and importance. And foremost among them all was the Kingdom of Koushal (now Oudh) whose dominion covered the area now occupied by the United

---

([1]) Rhys Davids--*Buddhist India*, p. 1.

Provinces. West and south of it, a number of small kingdoms maintained their independence. Eastward it had already extended its sovereignty over the Shakyas. To the south-east of Koushal lay another powerful kingdom of Magadh—now Bihar or the country to the east of Benares,—with its capital at Rajgrih, which in 300 B.C. vanquished Koushal. In Buddh's time the king of this country was Bimbeshwar (582-534 B.C.), who was succeded by his son Ajat Shatru.

To the south, there was the kingdom of Vamshas or Vatsas, with its capital at Koushambi on the Jumna near Allahabad, south of which lay the kingdom of Avanti, with its capital at Ujjain, ruled over by King Pajjot. These and a dozen or more towns constituted all that could be classed as the urban life in India. The rest of the country was dotted with villages. All the ruling families were, of course. Kshatriyas united by marriage. The clans into which they were divided have since lost their identity in other names.

They numbered about thirty: of which the Shakyas([1]) appear to have been as numerous (numbering a million) as they were powerful. Indeed, the clan name itself connotes power. The economic condition of the people then was little different from what one finds now in remote villages. From the remotest antiquity the villages in India have been autonomous in their internal management.

The village itself is now the subject of private ownership, but in the olden days this right was not recognized ; for the function of the owner now was then performed by the head-man who collected the rents, and generally acted as the *pater familias* to the villagers. All their internal affairs were regulated by custom and decided by the village Panchayat or Council of elders. Each village had its own tutelary village-god and its priest. The villages were inhabited by persons of all castes, who followed the occupations allotted to them by immemorial custom. The peasants cultivated their own fields, while those of a better class employed labourers, who became by custom

---

([1]) Sk. *Shak*—to hold power.

attached to the soil. These were the serfs of the soil. There was no slavery.([1])

But service akin to slavery was not unknown. The fact is that the fair-skinned Aryan immigrant, as he poured down into the country, found it sparsely populated by a dark-skinned aboriginal people whom he easily subdued and threw into the servile class.([2]) These aborigines belonged to the Mongolian stock and their squat " nose-less " faces aroused the contempt of the northern invader. Thus Vedic hymns abound in scornful references to them who are described as " gross feeders of flesh,'' " raw-eaters," " lawless," " disturbers of sacrifices "and" without gods." But they had all been subdued or driven into the forest long before the birth of Gautam.

Caste as such had not yet taken hold of the people who were divided into two main groups, Aryans and Aborigines ; and at the head of both stood the Kshatriyas or the nobles and the warriors, who had conquered the country which they ruled. These claimed descent from the Sun and the Moon, were proud of their lineage, " fair in colour, fine in presence, and stately to behold".([3]) Below them stood the Brahman, claiming descent from the sacrificing priests. They were, equally with the Kshatriyas, distinguished by high birth and clear complexion. Below them came the Vaishyas, who formed the bulk of the Aryan people engaged in trade and husbandry. And last of all came the Shudras, men of aboriginal descent, dark-skinned labourers, serfs and persons who were employed to perform or who followed menial occupations, such as tilling the soil, handicraft or service. Indeed, all spheres of low trade—such as barbers, potters, weavers, mat-makers, leather-makers—appear to have been relegated to this class,—whether they were or were not of Aryan extraction. Even below them stood another class—the Chandals and Pukkusas—who were treated as social outcasts.

---

(1) Megasthenes : *Arrian Ind. Ch. X*, *cited in* Rhys. Davids' *Buddhist India*, 262.
For his opinion *contra* See *Ib.* 55.

(2) Sk. " *Dasas* "—slaves.
(3) *Dialogues of Buddh* 1-148 ; *Vin.* II-4-160.

But caste, as we now understand it, had not then acquired the rigid immobility which it has since acquired. It was more or less vocational and flexible; and Manu himself classes the people into the twice-born and those falling under the head of commercial and servile classes. Inter-marriages between the twice-born appear to have been usual ([1]), though for the first marriage a Kshatriya must marry a Kshatriya and a Brahman a Brahman.([2]) But the laws of marriage were lax and love-matches known as *Gandharv* were recognized ([3]); and one could marry a person seized as a prisoner in battles([4]), and a liaison had the same effect as a marriage.([5]) But even regular inter-caste marriages were usual, and the marriage of a Kshatriya prince with a potter, a basket-maker, a florist or a cook did not entail loss of caste.([6]) A Brahman, though belonging to a priestly class, was suffered to trade([7]) or live by hunting and trapping([8]) or as a carpenter.([9]) They are frequently mentioned as engaged in agriculture([10]) and as hiring themselves out as cowherds and even goat-herds.

The fact is—that the Brahman then had a lower social standing than a Kshatriya, in comparison with whom he was spoken of as "low-born".([11]) His claim to pre-eminence, even if made, was not then accepted. On the other hand, the Kshatriya from whom he had selected all his favoured gods, *e.g.,* Ram and Krishna, showed their ascendency in the social hierarchy. Brahmans and Kshatriyas inter-dined as they do so still. But it appears that the earlier stages of the struggle for priestly supremacy had just begun in the life-time of Gautam.

([1]) *Manu,* III—4 (Sir Wm. Jones' *Tr.*), p. 40.
([2]) *Ib.* III—12, p. 41.
([3]) *Ib* III—32, p. 43.
([4]) *Ib* III—33, p 43
([5]) *Ib* III—34, p. 43.
([6]) *Jaatak,* II—5.
([7]) *Ib.* V—22.
([8]) *Ib.* II—200, VI—170.
([9]) *Ib.* IV—207.
([10]) *Jat,* V—257; Rhys Davids' *Buddhist India,* 60.
([11]) *Jaatak* V—257; Rhys Davids' *Buddhist India* 6: The superiority of the Kshatriyas was undisputed in the *Vedas.* For we are read in the *Shaspath-Brahman:*

"Brahmans formerly one only. It energetically created an excellent form, the Kshatriya, viz., those amongst the Gods who are powers: viz., Indra, Varun, etc.; hence nothing is superior to the Kshatriya: therefore the Brahman sits below the Kshatriya at the Raja-uya sacrific." (Muirs' *Old Sanskrit Texts* Vol. 1 p. 20). And in the same work elsewhere describing the graves of the dead it provides: "For a Kshatriya he may mark it is high as a man with up-stretched arms, for a Brahman reaching up to the mouth, for for a woman up to the hips, for a Vaishya up to the thighs, for a Shudra up to the knees." (*Satpath-Brahman* 44 S. B. E. 428, 429).

Literacy was not then general; but writing had been invented, the alphabet being borrowed and adapted from the Semitic sources; still, the writing of books had not yet commenced. All literature was committed to memory and the marvellous, indeed astounding, feats of memory were performed by those who made it their business to commit to memory a library of religious and philosophic literature. As an aid to memory this was consequently put in verse.

It is now agreed that the Sanskrit script was borrowed from the script of the Semitic tribes, who inhabited Babylon between which place and India there was a continued and extensive trade. This trade appears to have been carried on, both by land and sea,—by land, by way of the passes across Afghanistan, by sea, from ports on the west coast. The merchants were Dravidians who exported rice, ivory, apes and peacocks, frankincense and sandal-wood. The script appears to have been brought to India about the eighth or seventh century B. C. and the priests utilized it for drawing up memoranda on birch-bark, which was replaced by the leaves of the corypha and alipot palm, but never by clay-bricks as in Babylon. As writing was first utilized by the priestcraft, it soon became their monopoly till the Buddhists broke through it and widened its use by writing their canonical books equally upon metallic plates, stone-slabs and clay-moulds.

The Kharoshtri or Kashgar alphabet was introduced into India about 500 B.C. A Buddhist canonical book, written in that script with ink on birch-bark about the commencement of the Christian era, is still extant in the museums of Paris and Petrograd. But Ashoke's inscriptions on rocks and pillars, over 34 in number, are dated the third century B.C.

It is thus clear that knowledge in ancient India was disseminated by word of mouth. As there were professional memorists, who made it their duty to learn up and recite Sutras and books, so there were a large class of wandering hermits and peripetatic teachers of both sexes who made it their business to travel about eight months in the year with the sole object of engaging in conversational discussions on matters of religion and ethics, philosophy, Nature-lore, and mysticism. Like the Sophists in Greece, they naturally differed greatly in intelligence, earnestness and honesty. Some are described as "hair-splitters" and "eel-wrigglers"[1], others were money-making charlatans ; but, as a rule, they must have been earnest men ; for they were everywhere welcomed and honoured, and special lecture-halls and rest-houses were built for their accommodation and convenience. They met their equals or their rivals there and discussions and debates were held and heard by the populace. They all belonged to or followed the doctrine of some recognized school of thought and carried their distinctive flags, as the distinguished amongst them travelled with a considerable retinue. For instance, there were the "Mundak Sevaks" or the disciples of the shaveling, "Gotamaka," the followers of Gautam, that is, of Dev Dutt, Buddh's cousin and opponent, who denounced Buddh as an easy-going hermit who did not practise asceticism, "Tridandika"—or the bearers of the triple staff—Brahmans who opposed the Buddhists — "Devadhaminika" or followers of the orthodox gods—the Sanatanists, as we should call them now.

As these and many more traversed the whole country, the question arises—which language did they adopt as the vehicle of their expression? It is obvious that there was then no *lingua franca* for India. There is no *lingua franca* to-day. Nor was the Sanskrit any substitute for such a language—classical Sanskrit was not then in existence and the Brahmanical Sanskrit was not understood by the people. But the Prakrit had then come into existence. The languages which the people spoke were probably Prakrit, supplemented and varied by the local vernaculars, which must have been more akin to the various local dialects still surviving. The wanderers must have been then, as indeed, their confreres are to-day, multi-linguists, and all their discussions must have been carried on in Prakrit or in the local dialect. The fact that Ashoke's inscriptions are inscribed in Pali does not, of course, show that Pali was the

---

[1] *Dialogues of Buddh,* 1—37, 38.

spoken language, any more than the fact that the modern inscriptions in India are in English, shows that English is the language of the people.

Buddh had himself instructed his monks to preach to the people in their own dialect, which so far as the Koushal and Magadh countries were concerned, was probably Pali or Prakrit; also called Magadhi, from the country in which it was spoken (¹) : and Buddhism would never have conquered India with such giant strides as it did within the short period of a hundred years, were it not for the fact that both its matter and manner of teaching went straight to the hearts of the people who readily threw up their allegiance to Brahmanism and embraced this faith, which became and remained a state-religion in India for a period of more than three hundred years.

The history of India before the seventh century B.C. is obscure and mainly unreliable. The two great kingdoms of Koushal and Magadh were, however, then well-established. Of these, the first appears to have been more important, and extended on the north to the Himalayas. Its capital was Shravasti on the Rapti, probably represented by Sahet-Mahet. It was about 300 B.C. conquered by and became absorbed in the neighbouring kingdom of Magadh (South Bihar), which was the theatre for the exploits of early Jain and Buddhist religions. Magadh was founded about 642 B.C., by Sisunag, or Sheshnag (²), a chieftain of Benares, who established his capital at Girivraj (³) or old Rajgrah (⁴) among the hills of the Gaya district.

The first monarch of whom any authentic account is available is the fifth king Bimbeshwar (called Bimbisar or Shrenik) who ruled for 28 years (582-554 B.C.) and extended his kingdom by the conquest of Anga (now Bhagalpur and Monghyr districts). He had married a daughter of the powerful Licchavi clan. He founded a new town of Rajgrih (now Rajgir), which Gautam visited after his renunciation and near which were his

---

(¹) Childers' *Pali Dictionary, preface* XI f.n. (3) M'nayeff : *Pali Grammar* (*Fr. Ed.*) *Preface* XLII.

(²) *Sk.* "King of serpents."
(³) *Sk.* "Royal mountain."
(⁴) *Sk.* "Royal Palace."

4

two favourite resorts,—the hill known by its shape as the "Vulture Peak" and the "Venu Ban" (the Bamboo-grove).

Both Bimbeshwar and Prasannajit, King of Koushal were the lay disciples and constant patrons of Gautam ([1]). Bimbeshwar was succeeded in or about 554 B.C. by his son Ajit Shatru([2]) (Aj at Shatru or Kunika) who reigned for 27 years. He followed in the footsteps of his father and patronized Buddhism but appears later to have come under the influence of Devdutt and embraced Jainism,—which aroused the ire of the Buddhists who accused him of parricide. He built a fortress at Patali on the river Sone which afterwards grew into the imperial capital of Pataliputra (or modern Patna). His mother, as already stated, belonged to the Licchavi clan and he himself married a princess of the Kushal (Koushal) clan.

The Kingdom of Koushal ([3]) was, in the middle of the seventh century, great and at the height of its power. The kingdom of the Shakyas owed allegiance to its king. The ruler Mahakushal, controlled a tract of country extending from the Himalayas to the Ganges and from the Kushal and Ramganga rivers on the west to the Gandak on the east. Its further ambition was checked by the powerful confederation of the Licchavis, who were, however, defeated by Ajit Shatru, son of Bimbeshwar, who equally subjugated and annexed the kingdom of Kushal (Koushal).

The Licchavi clan who played an important part in Indian history had their Republic in Brij (Rijjis) (now the Mozaffarpur district of Bihar). Their capital was Vaisali. near Basarh, twenty miles to the north of Hajipur on the right bank of the Ganges, about 27 miles distant in a direct line from Pataliputra (modern Patna). Their country enjoyed the republican form of Government, being ruled by a council of notables presided over by an elected President (Nayak). They were allied by marriage with the Kushals on the one hand, and the king of Magadh on the

---

([1]) Vincent Smith's statement that King Bimbeshwar was a Jain appears to be erroneous—*History of India*, p. 45.

([2]) Sk. (" a "—*not*, " *Jit* "—conquered, " *Shatru* "—enemy) "invincible to his enemies." He is states to have got tired of his father's long reign and killed him. But the story is disbelived, being a pure invention by the Buddhists

([3]) Sk. (*Kushal—safe*), "a king who ensures the safety of his subjects."

other.   The wife of King Chandragupt I (322-298 B.C.), the
founder of the Gupt dynasty, was a Licchhavi princess, and
the clan is stated to have supplied a line of rulers in the Nepal
valley upto the seventh century A.D.

The Licchhavis are said to have been related to the Shakyas.
The Brahman writers regard them as degraded Kshatriyas; but
modern historians opine that they were all Mongolian hillmen
akin to the Tibetan and the modern Gurkha.   The evidence
upon which this opinion is based is the revolting practice, which
they are said to have followed,—of exposing their dead which
were sometimes hung upon trees, and their judicial procedure
in criminal cases was exactly the same as that of the Tibetan.   In
the first place, these facts are founded upon tradition which cannot be any guide for drawing a historical inference. In the second
place, it must be remembered that the Licchhavis have played
an important role in the early history of India, and their very
success may have led to the invention of a legend which the
Brahmanical writers would certainly have improved upon,if it
were true.   But whatever may be the origin of the Licchhavis,
the question is only one of historical interest.   But the question
whether Gautam Buddh was of Mongolian extraction—raises
an issue which interests the entire Buddhistic world.   The evidence upon which this opinion is hazarded is again tradition, and
even as such it is a *non sequitur.*   It is said that the first Tibetan
king was a Shakya belonging to another branch of the Gautam
family, and that he was a Licchhavi and that the Shakyas were
the Scythian or Turanian immigrants.(1)   Now as to the first
fact, if it be a fact, it does not support the conclusion ; since a pure
Kshatriya may have married into a Licchhavi family, but it does
not make the family a Licchhavi.   Then as to the Shakyas being
of Scythian origin, it is a tradition which persists in the case of
many Kshatriyas.   That they were not aborigines is clear, but
that they were Scythians or Turanians is merest conjecture,
and in its origin it may have been worse—an invention.

In order to determine the ethnological origin of a
race, tradition is never a safe guide unless it is supported

---

(1) V. Smith's *History of India*, pp. 48, 49,

by other facts. And what are the other facts here ?—
The Shakyas regarded themselves as a branch of the
Kushal (Koushal) family and were latterly their tributaries.
Now the Koushals are not classed as other than Kshatriyas
of Aryan descent, and so must be their kinsmen, the
Shakyas. Only recently it has been ascertained that the
dialects of Rajasthan bear a close resemblance to those spoken
along the Himalayas, not only in Nepal but as far west as Chumbi.
Rhys Davids thinks that this only shows that the ancestors of
the two must have been living close together when they began
their wanderings to the east and the south respectively. "Both
started from the Northern Punjab, and probably neither migration followed the Gangetic valley " [1]. Then again, the fact
that the Licchhavis exposed their dead,—is again a *non sequitur*,
since it is not shewn to be an exclusively Mongolian custom. The
ancient Persians did the same, as do the modern Parsis ; but no
one has yet suggested that they were Mongols. Indeed, if this
were the crucial test, it disproves the very theory it is sought to
prove, since the body of Buddh was never exposed, but cremat-
ed,—a purely Aryan method of disposal. Thirdly, Buddhism
being the religion of the Mongolian race, it is natural to claim the
Liberator as their own. But if this were a fact; the Brahmans,
who had invented caste and were anxious to preserve its purity,
would not have been the last to denounce the founder of the new
creed, which had crushed their religion, as a foreigner and a
Mongol for whom the Vedic sages had supreme contempt. The
fact that they treated him as a Kshatriya would be conclusive,
added to which we have the contemporaneous account of
his features which could only be those of a pure Aryan.

As already mentioned, the term " Kshatriya " had in those
days no greater significance than the term Brahman. Both
were more descriptive of the clan, rather than of the caste,which
had not then become crystallized into the rigid system it has
since become. Such is, at any rate, the view of those whose
authority is equally unquestionable. [2]

---

[1] *(1901)* *J. R. A. S. 808 :* cited in   [2] M. Williams—*Buddhism* p. 21
Rhys Davids' *Buddhist India.* pp. 32, 33.   Oldenberg—*Buddhism,* pp. 97, 98.

CHAPTER III.

It is impossible to understand the nature and extent of Buddh's contribution to the world's faiths and thought, without understanding the nature of the Faiths and Fallacies which confronted Buddh when he evolved his doctrine. As Gautam was a Hindu, and as such brought up in the shadow of that system, it is necessary to first examine the position of the Hindu in the seventh century before Christ.

The intensive study of Greek has naturally familiarized European scholars with the trend of Hellenic thought; but it is only during recent years that European scholars have found time to turn their attention to the language and literature of farther East. The reason for this neglect is not far to seek. With the advent of Christianity and its establishment in Europe, Europeans became naturally anxious to learn all about their religion; and as their Bible itself was written in Greek, they were attracted to the language and literature of that distinguished country. Its language had enriched the European languages, while its literature, at once varied and vast, gave to the scholar a double incentive of improving his language and enriching his mind. On the other hand, the literature of India was found embedded in a foreign tongue—a tongue the identity of which as a parent of the Aryan stock has only been established in comparatively recent times. And even then, its connection was remote and of no immediate practical value. Its literature was all embedded in that tongue, which was as difficult to master as it was difficult to understand. It was not, moreover, and it had been in all probability never,—a spoken tongue. The study of that language had, therefore, not the same practical value as the study of Latin or Greek. The literature to which it gave expression was the literature of an alien people, whom the Christians designated heathen, and to whom they ascribed opinions and views even more ridiculous than those held by the African savage or the Australian bushman.

The vast treasure-house of Oriental learning is, however, gradually being unearthed now; its principal books translated into European languages and a sober study made of its religious faiths. But, since Oriental scholars possess a religion of their own, they have not been always fair to the religions of other people ; nor have they appreciated the eternal truths to which some of them have given expression.

Unfortunately, of all such religions, Buddhism has been the greatest sufferer in this respect : for it is a religion, which impartial research has now proved to have been the parent of Christianity : not only as regards its main tenets, but also in the life and history of its founder and the organization of his Church.

And even where the two differ, as they do upon points incidental to their history, Buddhism possesses an advantage ; because its founder had placed before its history the torch-light of reason.

How far his reason has advanced the cause of Philosophy and how this ancient faith is able to withstand the shock of modern thought—is a question upon which we have to dwell at length in the sequel. For the present it would be sufficient if we examined the ground upon which the seed of Buddhism was sown.

It is now admitted that the Vedas are amongst the oldest of religious books in the world. European scholars are practically agreed that they must have existed in their present form from at least 1,200 to 1,000 B.C. (¹) " Scholars also agree that they contain a good deal of material even much older, and that the hymns in this last respect stand on the same footing as the Buddhist Pitakas or the Old Testament, or any other ancient Canon " (²). So Max Muller wrote that " the first germs of Upanishad doctrines go back at least as far as the Mantra period, which provisionally has been fixed between 1,000 and 800 B.C." ³ and which he describes as " among the most astounding productions of the human mind in any age and in any country "(⁴)

(¹) Rhys Davids *Buddhism* (*Am. Ed.*) p. 15.
(²) *Ib.* pp. 15, 16.

(³) *Upanishad 1 S.B.E. Introduction* LXVI.
(⁴) *Ib.* p. LXVII.

and of which Schopenhauer wrote : " In the whole world there is no study, except that of the originals, so beneficial and so elevating as that of the Upanishads. It has been the solace of my life, it will be the solace of my death."(¹)

The Upanishads which number close on 200 embody the Hindu system of Philosophy and Religion. For in those early days the difference between the two was neither well-marked, nor indeed even dimly appreciated; they were both treated as a part of the subject comprised in the term " Dharm,"(²) a large term which included duty of any kind—political, religious, ethical and social; it even included ceremonial observances and Law. Their views on religion were professedly rational. For had not the Upanishads said ?—" Now that light which shines above this Heaven, higher than all, higher than everything, in the highest world, that is the same light which is within man."(³)

Starting with this, it postulates the existence of God(⁴) and Soul(⁵). "The Infinite indeed, is below, above, behind, before, right and left,—it is indeed, all this." Now follows the explanation of the Infinite as the " I" : "I am below, I am above, I am behind, before, right and left—I am all this." Next follows the explanation of the Infinite as the Self : "Self is below, above, behind, before, right and left: Self is all this."(⁶) "To him who sees, perceives, and understands this, the spirit (Pran) springs from the Self, hope springs from the Self, memory springs from the Self, so do ether, fire, water, appearance, and disappearance, food, power, understanding, reflection, consideration, will, mind, speech, names, sacred hymns and sacrifices—aye, all this springs from the Self."(⁷) "The Self which is free from sin, the Self which is free from death and free from old age, from death and grief, from hunger and thirst, which desires nothing but what it ought to desire, and imagines nothing but what it ought to imagine, that it is which we must search out, that it is which we must

(1) Upanishad 1 S. B. E. Introduction p. LXI.
(2) Sk. " Dharm," lit. " Duty. "
(3) Upanishads III-13-8 ; 1 S.B.E. p. 47.
(4) Ib. I-9-4 ; 1 S. B. E. p. 17.
(5) Upanishads III-15-5 ; 1 S. B. E. p. 48.
(6) Ib. VII-25-1, 2 ; 1 S. B. E. pp. 123, 124.
(7) Ib. p. 124.

try to understand. He who has searched out that Self and
understands it, obtains all worlds and all desires"([1]).   "All
this, whatsover moves on earth, is to be hidden in the Self.
When thou hast surrendered all this, then thou mayst enjoy.
Do not covet the wealth of any man. Though a man may
wish to live a hundred years performing works, it will be thus
with him; but not in any other way : work will thus not cling to
a man.   There are the worlds of the Asuras covered with blind
darkness. Those who have destroyed their Self (who perform
works, without having arrived at a knowledge of the true Self)
go after death to those worlds. That One (Self), though never
stirring is swifter than thought.   The Devs (senses) never
reached it,—it walked before them.—Though standing still, it
overtakes the others who are running. Matarishvan (the
wind, the moving spirit) bestows powers on it. It stirs and
it stirs not: it is far, and likewise near. It is inside of all
this, and it is outside of all this. And he who beholds all
beings in the Self and the Self in all beings, he never turns
away from it. When to a man who understands, the Self
has become all things, what sorrow, what trouble can there be
to him who once beheld that unity?"([2])

It will be seen that the starting main motif of the
Upanishad philosophy was to establish the unity of the lower
Self, which we may call for convenience—the Ego, with the
universal Self,—which is another name for God. The merging
of one into the other was its ruling principle.

The Upanishads ([3]) are a part of the Vedas, being a part
of the Aranyaks, which began to be treated as the quintessence
of the Vedas and are, therefore, included in the term Shruti([4])
" or direct revelation from God." They profess to be the work
of no human hand. The Upanishads number about 200 and
promulgate diametrically opposing doctrines. This is due to
the fact that whenever a new school of thought came into exis-

---

[1] I. S B.E. p. 134.
[2] I S. B. E. pp. 311, 312.
[3] Sk. Upa-near and Sad—to sit , lit.
Sitting near (some one) to listen or for
worship: Max Muller Sk. Lit. (All.

Reprint) pp. 163, 164.
[4] Sk. Shrut " Heard (from God) as
opposed to Smrit " remembered " (i.e.
tradition).

tence, it composed an Upanishad of its own and tacked it on to
the older Upanishads.   One of the Upanishads declares that
knowledge of God cannot be obtained without a Messiah : "That
Divine Self is not to be grasped by tradition, nor by understanding, nor by all revelation; but by him whom He Himself chooses,
by him alone, is He to be grasped ; that Self chooses body as His
own."(1)   In another Upanishad (2) God is reduced to a mere
phantom: "Is Brahman the cause ? Whence are all born ? By
what do we live ? Where do we go ?   At whose command do
we walk after the law. in happiness and misery ?   Is Time the
cause, or Nature, or Law, or chance, or the elements ?   Is man
to be chosen as the source of all ? Nor is it their union, because
there must be independent Self, and even that independent Self
has no power over that which causes happiness and pain." The
Upanishads return no clear or consistent answer to what is God.
Some speak of Him as a masculine Self—implying that He is
personal (3), while others speak of Him in the neuter gender,
implying that it is merely a Power. (4)   In some books he is
spoken of merely as *Sat* or a Being (5), while in others he is called
Asat which is the negation of *Sat.*

Then as regards creation, the Upanishads support every
view, theistic, atheistic, agnostic, nihilistic, and pantheistic, and
the combination of some or all of them and many more, for which
no compendious expression exists at present.   The fact that
this would lead to hopeless contradictions and irreconcilable
differences does not seem to have perturbed the ancient thinkers,
who ascribed their differences to localities, rather than to the
rival schools of thought, of which there were no less than 1,180 ;
and as each school (6) claimed to have an Upanishad of its own,
there must have been as many Upanishads as there were schools.
That they could not have all come into existence *per saltum* is,
of course, obvious. But this much seems clear that the Vedant
Philosophy. by which all the schools were collectively known,
marked an epoch in the progress of human thought in which the

---

(1) *Katha Upanishad,* II—23 ; *See* J
S.B.E.
   (2) *Shvetavashtara—Upanishad*; *Sk. shvet*
—white, *ashva*—horse, and *tru*—to cross ;
" crossing by means of a white horse."

(3) *Bahvrichas.*
(4) *Taittiriyas.*
(5) *Chhandogyas.*
(6) *Called Shakha, Sk.* " a branch,"
" an off-shoo',"

liberty of human conscience had the widest field for display. In this respect the Hindu religion was at one time the most catholic in the world and presented a striking contrast with the other religious systems of the world.

That religion began with the Vedic ritual, in which the obtaining of earthly happiness, and afterwards bliss in the abode of Yama was obtainable only by the offer of correct sacrifices to the Gods. The second stage was reached, almost simultaneously or soon afterwards, when release from mundane existence by the absorption of the individual soul in the world-soul, through correct knowledge (not conduct yet), became the objective. Here, therefore, the sacrificial ceremonial became useless, and speculative knowledge all-important. [1] The Rigved, the oldest of the four Vedas, recognized a personal God, Prajapati,[2] and Purush [3]—Man, rather the world-man. This concept developed in the Upanishads into *Atman* or " Soul," or Brahm or Spirit of the universe which pervaded the universe. The words " *Brahm* " and " *Atman* " are found in the Vedas, but *Brahm* is there used to denote nothing more than " Prayer " or " Dev," while *Atman* in the Rig-ved means no more than "Breath," wind for instance, is spoken of as the *Atman* of *Varun*. The Upanishads gave it a wider, indeed, a newer meaning: " The Atman," it says, " is here all-pervading down to the tips of the nails. One does not see it any more than the razor hidden in its case or fire in its receptacle. For it does not appear as a whole. When it breathes, it is called breath, when it speaks, voice, when it hears, ear, when it thinks, mind. These are merely the means of its activities. He who worships the one or the other of them has not correct knowledge......one should worship it as the Self. For in it all these—breath etc. become one." [4]

In the old Upanishads the doctrine is first stated that the material word is an illusion, a *maya*—produced by Brahm as a conjuror (*mayin*). This is repeated in the later Upanishads, in which the whole doctrine of the Upanishads is

[1] Macdonnell's *Sanskrit literature*, p. 218.
[2] Sk. *Praja*—subjects, or created, *Pati*
—Lord or Creator; Lit. " Lord of creation."
[3] Sk. *Purush*—man.
[4] *Brihadaranyak* I—IV.

summed up in the famous formula—"That art thou," (¹) which
is explained to mean that the world-soul (*Atman*) and the individual soul are identical: "This whole world consists of it, that is
the Real, that is the Soul, that art thou, Shwaitketu" (²), "Even
as the smallest granule of millet, so is this golden Purush in the
heart......That Self of the spirit is my Self ; on passing from hence,
I shall obtain that self." (³) This is made clear by Yadnyavalkya
to his wife Maitreyi, as he was about to renounce the world and
retire to the forest : " As a lump of salt thrown into the water
would dissolve and could not be taken out again, while the water,
wherever tasted, would be salt, so is this great being, endless,
unlimited, simply composed of cognition. Arising out of these
elements, it disappears again in them. After death, there is no
consciousness." (⁴) In another passage of the same Upanishad,
we find the following : " Just as the spider goes out of itself by
means of its thread, as tiny sparks leap out of the fire, so from
the Atman issue all vital airs, all worlds, all gods all
beings." (⁵)

In other words, the prevailing doctrine of the Upanishads
is Pantheistic. Life is an emanation from Brahm into which
it returns. As clouds arise from the sea and fall into rivers,
and rivers flow into the sea and are lost, so is Atman; it comes
out of the Divine Atman and merges into it in the end.

Out of this monistic doctrine of the Divine Soul, per-
meating the universe, of which the human soul and the
creation is but an emanation, there arose the doctrine of the
transmigration of the soul, and with it the doctrine of Karm ;
both of which find places in the oldest Upanishads which
Buddh adopted as his own.

All the Upanishads allude to or describe these two
doctrines ; but the theory of transmigration is given in greatest
detail in the Chhandogya Upanishad, where it is thus described :
" This germ, covered in the womb, having dwelt there ten
months, or more or less, is born. When born, he lives what-

(¹) *Sk. "tat twam asi"*. (तत् त्वम् असि)
(²) *Chhandogya Upanishad*, VI—8-16.
(³) *Shatapath Brahman*, X—VI-3.
(⁴) *Brihadaranyak Upanishad* II—IV.
(⁵) *Ib.* II—1-20 ; To the same effect *Mandukya* III—11-8 ; *Chhandogya* VIII—7-12 ; *Brihadaranyak* III—VII.

ever the length of his life may be ; when he has departed, his friends carry him as appointed to the fire (of the funeral pyre) from whence he came, from whence he sprang. Those who know this, even though they still be Grihasths(¹), and those in the forest who follow faith and austerities, and of the Pari-Vrajaks, those who do not yet know the highest Brahman, go to light, from light to day, from day to the light-half of the moon from the light-half of the moon to the six months when the sun goes to the north, from the six months when the sun goes to the north to the year, from the year to the sun, from the sun to the moon, from the moon to the lightning. There is a person not human who does not go to the Brahman. That is Soma the king. But they, who living in a village practise a life of sacrifices, works of public utility, and alms, they go to the smoke, from smoke to night, from night to the dark-half of the moon, from the dark-half of the moon to the six months when the sun goes to the south. But they do not reach the year. From the months they go to the world of the fathers, from the world of the fathers to the earth, from the earth to the moon. Here they are loved by the Devas, yes, the Devas love them. Having dwelt there till their good works are consumed, they return again that way as they came, to the ether, from the ether to the air. Then the sacrificer, having become air, becomes smoke, having become smoke, he becomes mist. Having become mist, he becomes a cloud, having become cloud, he rains down. Then he is born as rice and corn, herbs and trees, Sesame and Beans. From thence the escape is beset with most difficulties. For whoever the person may be that eats the food, and begets off-spring, he henceforth becomes like unto them. Those, whose conduct has been good, will attain some good birth, the birth of a Brahman, or a Kshatriya, or a Vaishya. But those, whose conduct has been evil, will quickly attain an evil birth, the birth of a dog, or a frog, or a Chandal (²) ; on neither of these two ways those small

---

(¹) *Sk.* " Householders," as *opposed to*   (²) Lowest class of Shudra.
" *Vanprasths* "—forest-dwellers, ascetics.

creatures (flies, worms, etc.) are continually returning, of whom it may be said, ' live and die.' There is a third place."(¹)

The Vedant doctrine expounded dualism, but it developed in the leading Upanishads into pure Monism with the super-added doctrines of metempsychosis and Karm. The Upanishads likened human experience to a dream in which the visions appear real, but disappear as soon as the dreamer wakes. The reality of the world depends upon human consciousness. As soon as it disappears, what remains ? This doctrine was at one time upheld by Shankar (²); though later on he repudiated it and reverted to the realism of the Vedas. He said : " The perception is to be considered as similar to a dream and the like. The ideas present to our minds during a dream, magical illusion, a mirage and so on, appear in the two-fold form of subject and object, although there is all the while no external object ; hence, we conclude that the ideas of posts and the like which occur in our waking state are likewise independent of external objects ; for they are also simply ideas. If we be asked how, in the absence of external things, we account for the actual variety of ideas, we reply that the variety is to be explained from the impression left by previous ideas."

To all this we (the Vedantists) make the following reply : " The non-existence of external things cannot be main-tained, because we are conscious of external things. In every act of perception, we are conscious of some external thing corresponding to the idea, whether it be a post or a wall or a piece of cloth or a jar, and that of which we are conscious cannot but exist. Why should we pay attention to the words of a man who, while conscious of an outward thing through its approximation to his senses, affirms that he is conscious of no outward thing, and that no such thing exists, any more than we listen to a man who, while he is eating and experiencing the feeling of satisfaction, avers that he does not eat and does

---

(¹) *Chhandogya Upanishad* 1 V—9-1 *et seq*, 1 S.B.E. pp. 79-82.

(²) Also called Shankar Acharya (Shankar, the preceptor) ; flourished 800 A.D.

not feel satisfied ?   If the Buddh should reply that he does
not affirm that he is conscious of no object, but only that he is
conscious of no object apart from the act of consciousness,
we answer that he may indeed make any arbitrary statement
he likes, but that he has no arguments to prove what he
says.

"That the outward thing exists apart from consciousness— has necessarily to be accepted on the ground of the
nature of consciousness itself. Nobody when perceiving a
post or a wall is conscious of his perception only, but all men
are conscious of posts and walls and the like as objects of
their perceptions. That such is the consciousness of all men,
appears also from the fact that even those who contest the
existence of external things bear witness to their existence,
when they say that what is an external object of cognition
appears like something external. For they practically accept
the general consciousness which testifies to the existence of
an external world, and being at the same time anxious to
refute it, they speak of the external things as ' like something
external.' If they did not themselves at the bottom, ac-
knowledge the existence of the external world, how could
they use the expression, ' like something external ?' No one
says, ' Vishnumitra appears like the son of a barren woman.'
If we accept the truth, as it is given to us in our consciousness,
we must admit that the object of perception appears to us as
something external, not like something external.

" But, the Bauddh may reply, 'we conclude that the
object of perception is only like something external, because
external things are impossible.'

" This conclusion, we rejoin, is improper, since the possi-
bility or impossibility of things is to be determined only on
the ground of the operation or non-operation of the means
of right knowledge ; while, on the other hand, the operation
and non-operation of the means of right knowledge are not to
be made dependent on pre-conceived possibilities or impossi-
bilities. Possible is whatever is apprehended by perception

)r some other means of proof; impossible is what is not so apprehended. Nor, again, does the non-existence of objects follow from the fact of the ideas having the same form as the objects; for, if there were no objects, the ideas could not have the form of the objects, and the objects are actually apprehended as external. For the same reason (*i.e.*, because the distinction of things and ideas is given in consciousness), the invariable concomitance of idea and thing has to be considered as proving only that the thing constitutes the means of the idea, not that the two are identical.

"Moreover, when we are conscious first of a pot and then of a piece of cloth, consciousness remains the same in the two acts, while what varies is the distinctive attributes of consciousness; just as, when we see at first a black cow and then a white cow, the distinction of the two perceptions is due to the varying blackness and whiteness, while the generic character of the cow remains the same. The difference of the one permanent factor (from the two or more varying factors) is proved throughout by the two varying factors, and *vice versa*. Therefore, thing and idea are distinct.

"Further, if you say that we are conscious of the idea, you must admit that we are also conscious of the external thing.

"And if you rejoin that we are conscious of the idea on its own account because it is of a luminous nature like a lamp, while the external things are not so, we reply that by maintaining that the idea is illuminated by itself, you make yourself guilty of an absurdity, no less than if you said that fire burns itself. And at the same time you refuse to accept the common and altogether rational opinion that we are conscious of the external things by means of the idea different from the things! Indeed, a proof of extra-ordinary philosophic insight!"

The monistic doctrine of the Upanishads was combated by Kapil, the rationalistic founder of the Sankhya(1) philosophy,

---

(1) The doctrine is expounded in Book *XII Shanti Parva* 20-49 *Dutt's Tr.* pp. 432-434.

to which references are to be found only in the later Upanishads. Kapil preceded Buddh who followed and elaborated
his doctrine. Kapil is so mentioned by the Buddhistic
writers and frequent references to him occur in the Mahabharat, the twelfth book of which may be regarded as the
text-book of the system, since it has no Upanishad of its own,
nor has it left traces of any writing to which Kapil may have
committed his system. Indeed, the very existence of such a
person as Kapil is doubted, inspite of the unanimity with
which Indian tradition designates a man of this name, as the
author of certain Sutras. The oldest manual of the system, though
attributed to Kapil is, of course, a comparatively modern compi-
lation being composed only about 1,400 A.D. The oldest system-
atic treatise extant is the Sankhya-Karika of Ishwar Krishna,
translated into Chinese between 557 and 583 A.D. It men-
tions Panchashikh as the chief exponent of the system, who
may have lived about the beginning of the Christian era.

Kapil's philosophy, as described in the Mahabharat, is
relentlessly iconoclastic and essentially rational. Referring to
the miseries of life upon which the Vedantists dwell, he chaffed
them with the self-inflicted miseries of penance and sacrifice.
He maintains: "Direct evidence is the basis of both inference and the scriptures. The scriptures can be contra-
dicted by direct evidence. As to inference, its value is not
much. Do not reason on inference only, whatever may be
the subject. There is nothing else called individual soul
other than the body. The capacity to produce the banyan
seed possesses the capacity to produce leaves, flowers, fruits,
roots and bark....Likewise from the vital seed is produced the
body, with its attributes, the understanding, consciousness,
mind and other qualities. Two pieces of wood rubbed together
beget fire. Likewise the material body produces the mind and
its attributes of perception, memory, imagination, etc. As
the loadstone moves iron, likewise the senses are controlled
by the mind. Some hold that their re-birth is caused by
ignorance, the desire for acts, cupidity, carelessness, and bent
towards other vices. They say that ignorance is the soil,

acts form the seed that is placed in that soil. Desire is the water that causes that seed to grow.

In this manner they explain re-birth. They hold ignorance being ingrained in an imperceptible way ; one mortal body being destroyed, another originates at once from it ; and that when it is consumed by the help of knowledge, the destruction of existence follows, or the person attains to what is called liberation. This opinion is also mistaken. It may be asked that when the being that is thus re-born is a different one, in its nature, birth and objects of virtue and vice, why should it then be considered to be identical with the being that was ? Indeed, the only inference that can be made is that the entire chain of existence of a particular being is not really one of connected link. Then again, if the being that is the outcome of re-birth, is really different from what it was in a pristine existence, it may be asked what satisfaction does the person gain from the exercise of the spirit of charity, or from the acquisition of knowledge or of ascetic power ?— since the acts performed by one are to bear fruits upon another person in another state of existence. And the refutation of the doctrine would be—that one in this life may be rendered miserable by the acts of another in a pristine life, or having become miserable may again become happy. By witnessing, however, what actually takes place in the world, a proper conclusion may be drawn regarding the unseen."(1)

" The separate consciousness that is the outcome of re-birth, is different from the consciousness that had preceded it in a pristine existence. The way, however, in which the appearance of that separate consciousness is explained by that theory is not at all consistent or reasonable. The consciousness was the very opposite of eternal, being only transitory, extending as it did, till the dissolution of the body. That which had an end cannot be considered as the cause for the production of a second consciousness appearing after the end. If again, the very loss of the previous consciousness be considered as the cause of the production of the second

---

(1) *Mahabharat*, Dutt's Tr. pp. 322, 323.

5

consciousness, then when the death of a human body is caused by a heavy bludgeon, a second body would originate from the body that is thus deprived of animation.

"Again, their doctrine of annihilation is subject to the objection that extinction will become a revolving phenomenon like that of the seasons, or the year, or the yuga, or heat, or cold, or agreeable or disagreeable objects.

"If, for avoiding these objections, the followers of this doctrine hold the existence of a Soul that is permanent and with which each new consciousness is attached, they again subject themselves to the new objection that that permanent substance, by being overcome with decrepitude and with death that causes destruction, may in time be itself weakened and destroyed. If the supports of a palace are weakened by time, the mansion itself is sure to fall down in the end.

"The senses, the mind, wind, blood, flesh, bones, one after another meet with destruction and enter each time its own productive cause.

"If again the existence of an eternal Soul is held—which is immutable, which is the refuge of the understanding, consciousness, and other similar attributes, and which is dissociated from all these,—such an assertion is subject to a serious objection; for then all that is usually done in the world would be meaningless, especially with reference to the attainment of the fruits of charity and other religious acts. All the injunctions in the Shrutis regarding those acts, and all acts connected with the conduct of men in the world, would be equally meaningless; for the Soul being dissociated from the understanding and the mind, there is no one to enjoy the fruits of good acts and Vedic rites([1])."

Kapil denies the existence of a supreme God as creator or ruler of the universe. He denied that there was any cogent evidence about the existence of God ; still less was there any evidence that He had created and ruled the universe. He pointed to the origin of misery and pain, cruelty and injustice,

---

([1]) *Mahablarat : Shanti Parv Bk.* XII—§27.

suffering and pain, decay and death which were unjustly
apportioned and unequally suffered,—which a just and bene-
volent God could not tolerate, and for which, if He existed,
He could not escape the reproach of cruelty and partiality.
His existence must then be ruled out as beyond the pale of
reason—what then remains ? How is the existence of the universe
to be accounted for ? His theory of cosmogony strictly follows
the line of inductive ratiocination. His argument proceeds
from the known to the unknown till the ultimate cause is
reached, beyond which he refuses to go, and those who do, he
attacks by the same weapon of reason by which he has built
up his system. To him the world is real,because it is proved
by apperception. That world is eternal and has been and is
developing, according to certain laws, out of primordial
matter([1]). It has had no beginning and it will have no end—
though it will dissolve into primitive matter, alternating with
evolution, existence and dissolution.

But what becomes of the Soul, while matter is undergoing
its pre-destined course through these three stages ?

Kapil maintains that the Soul or *Purush* remains only a
passive spectator. It is the Supreme Spirit into which all
individual consciousness merges, just as the rivers flow into and
are lost in the sea. But just as the drops that make the river
never lose their identity, even though they become merged in
the sea, so the individual soul, if it may be so called, does not
lose its identity, though it is blended with the cosmic soul.

"Tho psychology of the Sankhya system is specially
important. Peculiarly interesting is its doctrine— that all mental
operations, such as perception, thinking, willing, are not performed by the soul, but are merely mechanical processes of
the internal organs, that is to say, of matter. The soul itself
possesses no attributes or qualities, and can only be described
negatively. There being no qualitative difference between souls,
the principle of personality and identity is supplied by the
subtle or internal body, which, chiefly formed of the inner

(1) *Sk.* " *Prakriti* or " *Prad han,*"—primitive matter.

organs and the senses, surrounds and is made conscious by the soul. This internal body, being the vehicle of merit and demerit, which are the basis of transmigration, accompanies the soul on its wanderings from one gross body to another, whether the latter be that of a god, a man, an animal, or a tree. Conscious life is bondage to pain, in which pleasure is included by the peculiarly pessimistic system. When salvation, which is the absolute cessation of pain, is obtained, the internal body is dissolved into its material elements, and the soul, becoming finally isolated, continues to exist individually, but in absolute unconsciousness."[1]

Kapil explains it by postulating the existence of matter and soul. According to him, matter is unconscious but contains within itself the power of evolution (in the interests of souls, which are entirely passive during the process) while Karm alone determines the course of that evolution.

The rigours of this logical system appear, however, to have been relaxed by a method adopted for bridging the gulf between the seen and the unseen. For both the Sankhya and the Vedant appear to have agreed on the practice of Yoge[2], as enlarging the vision beyond the material horizon. The practice of Yoge or intense meditation was itself the survival of the Vedic tapas[3], which was a form of asceticism combined with penance. It is not clear whether Kapil himself recognized Yoge as the gate-way to higher knowledge, but it was the theme of the grammarian Patanjali, who expounded it in his Yoge Shastra, written about 200 B.C. The fact that this work became known as the Sankhya Pravachan, the name given to the later Sankhya Sutras, shows its close association with and recognition by Kapil's school as a part of their system and they are so treated in the Mahabharat. But the futility of the practice of Yoge without God, which is still regarded as the most effective means of acquiring occult knowledge and super-natural power,—must have become apparent to its early protagonists; and Patanjali had to introduce in his system the

---

[1] Mac. Donnell's *Sanskrit Literature*, "Joining" or "union" (of matter with spirit).
392.
[2] *Sk. Yug* (*Lat. Jugam*—a yoke.)   [3] *Sk. Tap*—heat, warmth ; pain, suffering.

doctrine of a personal God, though he clearly saw its irreconcilable nature, and, therefore, relegated his *sutras* dealing with God to a place unconnected with his treatise. It was probably a forced concession, intended to stem the tide of speculative reaction. For, in his treatise Patanjali still adhered to the orthodox Sankhya doctrine—that the final aim of man was the absolute isolation of the soul from matter, and not as in the Vedantic doctrine,—the union with or absorption with God. Nor are the individual souls here derived from the" Special Soul or God, but are like the latter—without a beginning." ([1])

As in tapas—suffering without concentration, so in Yoge—concentration without suffering—was the chief aim. Both, however, were believed to be conducive to spiritual exaltation, raising the Yogi above the narrow surroundings of the material world and vesting him with a higher power in closer association with God. The Yogi being an aspirant for wresting the secrets of the universe denied to man, was interrupted in his Dhyan or meditation by the powers of Evil, who by seduction, enticement, force or fraud, sought to disturb him by distracting his attention. This fact accounts for the legendary episodes connected with Mar's interference with Buddh in his meditation.

That Buddh was a firm believer in the efficacy of Yoge is clear from the tenour of his earlier life. From the moment of his great renunciation till the day of his deliverance, Buddh was in search of a key to true knowledge. He only found it in Yoge. But Buddh believed in Yoge as a mental telescope; he did not believe in its efficacy beyond chastening the mind by freeing it from material distractions. It was the pre-Buddhistic view. But in later time and by Patanjali, Yoge was given a special significance and was maintained to be the chief means of salvation.

What is Yoge, then? Bhishm, the great sage, has himself explained it. "Freed from the influence of all pairs of opposites (such as, heat and cold, joy and sorrow etc.) ever exercising them in their own pure state, freed from attachment, never ac cepting anything in gift, they live in places separated from their wives and children, without others with whom disputes may arise, and favourable to perfect tranquillity of heart. There, restraining speech, such a person sits like a piece of wood, killing all the senses, and with mind immersed in the Supreme Self by the help of meditation. He has no perception of sound through the ear, no perception of touch through the skin, no perception of form through the eye, no perception of taste through the tongue."[1]

Lest this state of concentration may send the Yogi to sleep, the rules to keep the consciousness awake are provided. The Yogi is to inhale, suspend and expel the breath through each nostril alternatively ; then again suspend breath, inhale it to the utmost and exhale it slowly, the eyes are to rest on the tip of the nose and the Yogi must sit in a squatting posture, which he must retain through the performance of his exercise.

The practice of Yoge became popular with the theory—that the soul, when weighed down by the consciousness of material things, cannot rise to higher things; that, therefore, it must be freed from the fetters of mundane consciousness and concentrated upon the thought of Brahm. It would then reach the goal it aspires to reach. Yoge is then the suspension of the ordinary functions of life. It produces temporary death, and as life is the barrier to the union of the two souls—individual and divine,—the Yogi attains that region of heavenly bliss by making himself dead to his earthly surroundings.

The veil being thus raised, he sees the unseen and acquires the larger powers possessed by the larger soul.

It is in the cradle of this system that Buddhism was born. India was not then in communication with the outer world. Confined by the barriers of land and sea, it was left to its own resources to devise its own life. Nevertheless its philosophic system, if purged of the fable and allegories by which it is overlaid, would compare favourably with the trend of contemporary thought elsewhere.

---

[1] *Mahabharat, Shanti Parv Bk.* XII Ch. 145 § 3-6 ; 290.

The only other country that can at all compare with the depth and profundity of the Indian thought is Greece and both place knowledge as the means to salvation. It must be remembered that Socrates was born in 469 B.C., that is to say, more than 500 years later than the Vedantists. The Greek philosophy begins with Thales (640-550 B.C.), who was a contemporary of Buddh, as he himself was a contemporary of Crœsus and Solon. The quintessence of his thought is contained in the following maxim : " The principle (the *first*, the primitive ground) of all things is water, all comes from water, and to water all returns"(1). His conception of life was founded on observation and experience. He knew that the seed of life cannot grow without water and he concluded that water was, therefore, the beginning and the end of all things. His disciple, Anaximander, maintained that "primitive matter was the eternal, infinite, indefinite ground, from which, in order of time all arises, and into which all returns".

His own disciple, Anaximenes, conceived the principle of the universe to be the " unlimited, all-embracing ever-moving air," from which, by rarefaction (fire) and condensation (water, earth, stone) everything else is formed. His theory rested probably on the fact that he found the air surrounding the globe as necessary to sustain life. Pythagoras (540-500 B.C.) originated the theory of numbers. His view, or rather the view of his school, was that since all things existent had form and measure, the only quality by which they can be identified and distinguished was the number, which was consequently the vital principle of the universe. The Eleatics under Xenophon reduced their system to the fundamental maxim: "Only being is, and non-being is not all". This was the natural deduction from the Pythagorean multiplex system and postulated existence to be compatible only with dividedness in space and successiveness in time. The system was developed by Parmenides and Zeno who propounded the monistic doctrine that being and thought were one ; and so were the body and the soul. He

---

(1) Shwegler's *History of Philosophy* (Sterlings' Trans)9.

regarded origin and decease, perishable existence, multiplicity and diversity, change of place and alteration of quality, all an illusion or " non-being "—what Vedantist had called, a thousand years before him, Maya or a mirage. Zeno, who influenced Plato, developed the same thought by denying the evidence of senses and reduced all beings into " One " which he vaguely defined in the Vedantic sense.

Heraclitus held to the doctrine of eternal change, the alternation of life and death, and that the one principle of life is dualism typified by the dualism of life and death. Socrates said of him. "That what he understood was excellent, what not, he believed it to be so ; but that the book required a tough swimmer". Leucippus and Democritus (460 B.C.) founded the Atomic theory of Nature, holding that the alternate conjunctions and disjunctions of primordial atoms constituted the universe. His theory, like that of Kapil, was atheistic. But while India welcomed the freedom of thought, Greece banished all free-thinkers like Anaxagoras (born about 500 B.C.) and Protagoras (440 B.C.) who had to leave Athens because they ascribed all Nature to be the mechanical product of cosmic energy. To him mind was a mere hypothesis. The Sophists first led by Protagoras (440 B.C.) revived the doctrine of illusion and denied the objective existence of matter. To them " man is the measure of all things".

He closed the first period of Greek Philosophy. The second begins with Socrates (469-399 B.C.) and was further developed by his disciple—Plato, and the latter's disciple—Aristotle. Socrates never professed to propound any constructive doctrine of his own. His philosophy is, therefore, only an abstraction of his character as expressed in casual conversation. He too was a martyr to his own opinions, for as it is well-known, he was condemned for blasphemy and seducing the young.

Socrates' contribution to philosophy is, like Bacon's *Novum organum*, the introduction of a new method for ascertaining the truth. He had lived his life, removing the cobwebs from the minds of the young Athenian. His own life was a vivid illustration of his own teaching. For the rest, he shared the popular belief in the supremacy of the gods and the existence of heaven and hell to reward the virtuous and punish the guilty. He was a believer in the doctrine of Karm, for he consigned to Tartarus those who had committed great crimes, while those who had sufficiently purified themselves by philosophy were to live " without bodies, throughout all future time, and shall arrive at habitations yet more beautiful than these, which it is neither easy to describe, nor at present is there sufficient time for the purpose."(¹)

But he was not quite certain that there was such a thing as soul, though he thought it " most fitting to be believed, and worthy the hazard for one who trusts in its reality; for the hazard is noble and it is right to allure ourselves with such things as with enchantments." (²) Socrates was then an agnostic in these matters, but reason failing, he turned to faith to make life agreeable.

But though Socrates founded no school of thought, his disciple—Plato (429-347 B.C.) did. In effect, it is but a development of the Eleatic idealism, in which he denies the existence of matter, but maintains the reality of its idea, that is to say, its subjective conception as distinct from its objective reality.(³) He sees an undivine natural principle in the world(⁴) and a malevolent world-soul.(⁵) His view on the creative energy is not well-developed and is, indeed, not even consistent ; for he regarded it either as an emanation of the absolute spirit, or as a verity of a self-existent eternity, or as nothing but a sub- jective conception and an illusion. " But his main purpose was to combat the theory of dualism and for this purpose he denied the existence of matter, agreeing in this respect with the monistic Vedantic view of Maya, but with the advantage all on the side of the Vedantist; first, because he had anticipated Plato by a 1,000 years ; and secondly, because the Vedantist view is explained

<hr>

(¹) *Phœdo* I—Plato's collected works (Bohu), 123.
(²) *Phœdo* 1—Plato's collected works (Bohu), 123.
(³) *Parmenides*.
(⁴) *States* 268.
(⁵) *Laws* X 896.

with a greater assurance and in greater detail, and it has not to make a futile struggle against dualism." ([1])   Plato's idealism was extended to his conception of God whom he regarded as also an " idea of the Good."   His system did not allow of a personal God ; for, his absolute idea being universal, his God must be equally so.   But Pantheistic though his system led up to be, Plato, like his Master, subscribed to his belief in the traditional faith in God or gods.

The fact is that Plato's philosophy and his religion were two things apart, and he never attempted to reconcile them. Plato believed in the individual soul which possessed the same characteristics as the universal soul.   Through reason it partakes of the divine soul ; but so long as it resides in the body, it partakes of its character and, being subject to sensuous feelings and greeds, it descends from the celestial to the earthly, from the immortal to the   mortal sphere. Body and soul naturally control each other.   The pure soul, which has withstood the proof of association with the corporeal world untainted, returns at death into the state of blissful repose, returning however, after a time to the body. The ultimate end of the soul is its final liberation from its corporeal companionship, which can only be attained by the practice of virtue.   The soul which had given itself up to sense, incurs the penalty of migration into new bodies, it may be—even into lower forms of existence, from which it is delivered only when, in the course of time, it has recovered its purity.

All this sounds as if it were an exposition of Buddhism. But it is not.   It is pure Platonism and one is curious to know if there was possibly any exchange of ideas between the disciples of the Eastern sage and of the Western idealist ; for, the Platonic theory of re-incarnation looks like the paraphrase of the Buddhistic doctrine, between which and Platonism there is much more in common.

The Platonic doctrine received a vigorous attack at the hand of his versatile disciple—Aristotle (384-322 B.C.), founder of the

---

[1] Schwegler's *History of Philosophy* (*Sterling's Tr.*) 80.

Peripatetic school, who may be said to have emulated Kapil in melting all theories down in his crucible of rationalism.   As a philosopher, he was an empirist and denounced Plato's ideas— as only " things of sense, immortalised and eternalised," sterile and as offering no explanation for existence.   His system cor- responds with that of Kapil in that he recognised the existence of an absolute passive spirit and of the reality of matter and in the case of man, soul as its animating principle.   Aristotle rejects the monism of Plato and would equally reject the monism of the Vedantic sages.   To him the human soul is a *tabula rasa*, upon which are inscribed the impressions of its impact with matter. But as the human soul is powerless to act without matter, so is the divine soul.

His ethics lays emphasis upon the exercise of virtue, and not merely upon its knowledge.   Happiness, to him lies in a perfect activity in a perfect life. Aristotle was the last of the Greek philosophers. After him their productive power declined and became exhausted with the decline of their national life.   Zeno (B.—340 B.C.) founded the school of Stoics. To them, God was the active and formative power of matter : the world was its body, and God, its soul. In them there was a revival of the monistic doctrine, though in a different form. God ruled the world.   All in it is equally divine, for the divine power equally pervaded all.   Everything was subject to His immutable laws, and this law rewarded the good and punished the wicked.   Their ethics, expressed in the maxim—"Follow Nature," or "Live in agreement with Nature," subjected human acts to the rationality and order of universal Nature :   " The touch-stone of virtue is reason."

Little need be said of Epicurus (342-270 B.C.), founder of the Epicurean school, whose philosophy was practical and defined to be an activity which realises a happy life through ideas and arguments.   To them the supreme joy is the joy of spirit, produced by the imperturbable tranquillity of the wise man,—in the feeling of his inner worth, of superiority to the blows of fate. To them the tranquillity of the soul, the impassability of mind, was all in all, though, unlike the cynics, they did not shun pleasures of the moment. They know nothing of the moral destiny of man. To them God exists in the empty inter-spaces, in human forms without human-bodies, in perfect bliss. with no duty towards man. This practically closes the last chapter in Grecian philosophy.

Even a casual reader will easily discern the close parallelism between the Indian speculation and Greek thought. It is not easy to speculate how far the two systems were inter-dependent ; but the fact that Indian religious system is several centuries older, makes one feel whether one did not influence the other. But whether it is so or not, the fact remains that the structure of Buddhism was built upon the foundation of Indian Philosophy and that it owes nothing to foreign influences. On the other hand, there is the historical data for inference that in the fourth century B.C., when Alexander visited India, he carried along with him the gems of Buddhist thought and that in his passage back, he acted as the carrier of the new gospel which Buddh had preached and the superb morality which his religion had evolved for the happiness of mankind.

This is the end of this publication.

Any remaining blank pages are for our book binding
requirements and are blank on purpose.

To search thousands of interesting publications like this one,
please remember to visit our website at:

http://www.kessinger.net

www.ingramcontent.com/pod-product-compliance
Lightning Source LLC
LaVergne TN
LVHW091941060326
832903LV00043B/12